GUJARATI 101 FOR EVERYONE:
Speak, Understand, Connect

Translations in easy-to-read English!

Image by Freepik

This is my family. – Aa maro parivar chhe.

How To Use This Book

This book is designed for anyone wanting to understand and speak Gujarati. The easy English to Gujarati translations with English syllables and pronunciations are designed to help beginners. Caregivers may read the sentences to their younger children. Older children should be able to read the translations on their own when they know the pronunciations!

Each page represents a category of daily conversations. The content will have English lines followed by their Gujarati translations written in English letters for easier pronunciation.

Copyright © 2025 Drashti Patel (Pathways and Paychecks). All Rights Reserved. No part of this book may be reproduced, distributed, or transmitted in any form or by any means, including photocopying, recording, or other electronic or mechanical methods, without the prior written permission of the author, except in the case of brief quotations embodied in critical reviews and certain other noncommercial uses permitted by copyright law. Images and illustrations are generated or borrowed from Canva, Microsoft Designer and Freepik.
For permissions, contact: pathwaysandpaychecks@gmail.com

Table of Contents

How To Use This Book 3

Author's Note 6

What is Gujarati? 7

Basic Words & Greetings 9

Common Objects 11

Common Action Verbs 13

Question Words/Phrases 15

People & Relations (Immediate) 17

People & Relations (Extended) 19

Prepositions 21

Daily/Common Phrases (1) 23

Daily/Common Phrases (2) 25

School and Learning 27

Counting Numbers (1-10) 29

Counting Numbers (11-20) 31

Counting Numbers (0-100) 33

Common Foods 35

Dining Table Phrases 37

Playing Outside 39

Conversations with Friends 41

Traveling in a Taxi/Rickshaw 49
Traveling (Airport) 51
Asking for Help 53
Hobbies and Interests (1) 55
Hobbies and Interests (2) 57
Birthday 59
Body Parts 61
Festivals 63
Describing the Weather 65
Animals 67
Colors and Shapes 69
Saying Goodbye 71
End Note 72

Author's Note

To keep things simple, this book does not go in details of the grammar rules.

In Gujarati the sentence structure generally adheres to a Subject – Object – Verb (SOV) arrangement.

[Handwritten annotations: "I, we / What the sentence is about" under Subject; "receiver of the action" under Object; "Action is, was, were" under Verb]

Grammar: Nouns are categorized by gender (masculine, feminine, neuter), number (singular/plural), and case distinctions (nominative, oblique/vocative, and locative).

Pronouns: Various forms are available depending on the level of formality and familiarity.

Verb Conjugation: Verbs exhibit significant inflection according to tense, aspect, mood, as well as the gender and number of the subject.

Reference: Patel, Pinkesh & Maurya, Sandeep & Maurya, Khushbu & Chaudhary, Gaurav. (2016). Gender and Number Identification for Gujarati word : Rule-Based Approach. National Journal Of System and Information Technology. 9. 77-82.

What is Gujarati?

Gujarati is an Indian language native to the Indian state of Gujarat and spoken predominantly by the Gujarati people. While Gujarati has several dialects, this book contains the simplest translations and pronunciations spoken by most Gujaratis around the world!

A language is best learned by immersion, so start talking, reading, and watching shows/movies!

<u>Note:</u> The Gujarati barakhadi contains 48 letters, some of which don't have an equivalent pronunciation with English alphabets. E.g. "Water" in Gujarati is "પાણી" and will be written as "Pani". "We/us" which is "આપણે" will be written as "Aapne".

"Fox" in Gujarati is "શિયાળ" and will be written as "Shiyaal (/Shiyaad)" to help with the pronunciation.

(I will soon work on an 'Audible' version to make it easier for new beginners to understand and practice their pronunciations!)

Image by studio4rt on Freepik

How are you? - Kem chho?
Hello! - Kem chho!

Every word in this lavage is either in a buddy system, or threes ie ~~[scribbled out]~~ *Kar-ei-ke-ya*

Basic Words & Greetings

==(Chill version)== Th-may Ka-va chho
                    Dear person How are you? ==(more respectful)==
                                                              elder, guest
- **Hello – Kem chho**
  + How are you

- **Goodbye – Aavjo**   • "ōw-joe"

- **Yes – Ha**

Hello	Kem
are you good	— chho
are you enjoying	Ma-ja-ma?
life/doing well?	
- **No – Na**

  | I'm doing well / living / enjoying life | — Majama chew |

- ~~**Please – Krupa karine**~~
  Cru-pa car-na

- ~~**Thank you – Aabhar**~~ (No one uses this)

- **Sorry – Maaf karjo**

  Please Forgive (Please do this) — Maf car-jo   swa-gut chay

- **Welcome (I welcome you) – Swagat chhe**
  (when a new guest coming to house)
  "welcome to my home"

Gu-ja-ra-ti

9

What do you see outside the window?
- Tamne/ Tane bari ni bahar shu dekhay chhe?

Which book do you want to read?
- Tamare kai chopdi vaanchvi chhe?

How many books are on the table?
- Table par ketla pustako chhe?

Common Objects

- Book – Pustak/Chopdi
- Water – Pani
- Food – Khavanu/ Jamvanu/ Bhojan
- Home – Ghar
- Car – Gaadi
- Chair – Khurshi
- Door – Darwajo
- Keys – Chaavi
- Window – Bari

Sit, eat, drink – Besvu, khavu, pivu

Common Action Verbs

- Eat – Khavu *Kha-va-new*
- Drink – Pivu *Pee-va-new*
- Sleep – Unghvu/ Suvu *Sue(or)ung -va-new*
- Walk – Chalvu *Chal-vaa-new*
- Run – Dodvu *Duhor-va-new*
- Sit – Besvu
- Stand – Ubha Rehevu
- Talk – Vaat Karvi
- Put – Mukvu
- Take – Levu
- Give – Aapvu
- Read – Vaanchvu
- Write – Lakhvu

Who – Kon?
What – Shu?
Why – Kem?

Question Words/Phrases

- Who? – Kon?
- What? – Shu?
- Where? – Kya?
- When? – Kyare?
- How? – Kevi rite?
- Who are you? – Tame kon chho?
- What happened? – Shu thayu?
- Where did the car go? – Ae gaadi kya gayi?
- When will you come back? – Tame pachha kyare aavsho?
- How did you do that? – Tame ae kai/kevi rite karyu?

Designed by pikisuperstar / Freepik

It's my aunt's wedding! - Mari masi/foi/kaki na lagna chhe!

We went to my aunt's house - Ame masi/foi/kaki/mami na ghare gaya hata.

The wedding had delicious food! - Lagna ma swadisht jamvanu hatu!

People & Relations (Immediate)

- Mother – Mummy / Ma
- Father – Pappa / Pitaji
- Brother – Bhai
- Sister – Bahen
- Grandmother – Dadi / Nani
- Grandfather – Dada / Nana
- Son – Dikro
- Daughter – Dikri
- Wife – Patni
- Husband – Pati

I have 2 brothers and 1 sister.
– Mare be bhai ane ek bahen chhe.

People & Relations (Extended)

- Mom's sister – Masi
- Mom's sister's husband – Masa
- Mom's brother – Mama
- Mom's brother's wife – Mami
- Dad's brother – Kaka or Mota pappa
- Dad's brother's wife – Kaki or Moti mummy
- Dad's sister – Fiya / Fai / Foi
- Dad's sister's husband – Fua

Let's read something!
- Chalo kaik vaanchiye!

Prepositions

- On – Upar
- In – Andar
- Under – Neeche
- Near – Najik
- Between – Vachche
- Behind – Paachhal (/Paachhad)
- In front of – Saame
- Next to – Baajuma
- With – Saathe
- Without – Vina / Vagar
- About – Vishe
- For – Maate
- From – Maathi
- To – Sudhi
- Inside – Andar
- Outside – Bahar
- Above – Upar
- Below – Neeche
- Before – Pehla
- After – Pachhi

What am I thinking?
– Hu shu vicharu chhu?

Daily/Common Phrases (1)

- Where is my toy? – Maaru ramakdu kya chhe?

- What is your name? – Tamaru / taru naam shu chhe?

- It is on the table. – Te table par chhe.

- Where are you going? – Tame kya jao chho?

- I am hungry. – Mane bhukh lagi chhe.

- Go to your room. – Tara/Tari room ma ja.

- My name is Priya. – Maru naam Priya chhe.

**Please give me the paint brush.
– Mane paint brush aapo.**

Daily/Common Phrases (2)

- Wake up. – Uthi jao/ Utho/ Jago.
- Brush your teeth. – Dant saaf (/brush) karo.
- Comb your hair. – Vaal olo (/Vaad odo).
- Take a bath. – Naahi lo.
- Eat the food. – Khavanu khao/ Jamvanu jamo.
- Go to sleep. – Sui jao.
- Come here. – Ahiya aavo.
- Go there. – Tya jao.
- Give it to me. – Mane aapo.

I like to write!
– Mane lakhvu gamey chhe!

What are you writing?
- Tu shu lakhe chhe? /Tame shu lakho chho?

School and Learning

- I need my book. – Mane maaru pustak (/maari chopdi) joiye chhe.

- What is today's homework? – Aaj nu ghar kaam (/homework) shu chhe?

- Mom, can you help me? – Mummy, mane madad karsho?

- Let's play together. – Chalo, saathe ramiye.

- My favorite subject is math. – Maaro gamto vishay ganit (math) chhe.

- I like going to school! - Mane school javu gamey chhe!

**Let's count 1 to 10
- Ek thi das ganiye!**

**It's 9 am right now.
– Hamna savarna nav vagya chhe.**

Counting Numbers (1-10)

- One – Ek
- Two – Be
- Three – Tran
- Four – Chaar
- Five – Panch
- Six – Chha
- Seven – Saat
- Eight – Aanth
- Nine – Nav
- Ten – Das

**How many fingers am I holding?
– Mae ketli anglio(/angdio) upar kari?**

Counting Numbers (11-20)

- Eleven – Agiyar

- Twelve – Baar

- Thirteen – Ter

- Fourteen – Choud

- Fifteen – Pandar

- Sixteen – Sol (/Sod)

- Seventeen – Sattar

- Eighteen – Adhar

- Nineteen – Oganis

- Twenty – Vees

Image by brgfx on Freepik

**What number does my balloon have? –
Mara fugga par kayo aankdo (/number) chhe?**

Counting Numbers (0-100)

- Zero – Shunya
- Ten – Das
- Twenty – Vees
- Thirty – Tris
- Forty – Chalis
- Fifty – Pachaas
- Sixty – Saahith
- Seventy – Sittaer
- Eighty – Aensi
- Ninety – Nevu
- One Hundred – Ekso/ So

I love eating okra! – Mane bhinda bahu bhave chhe!

Common Foods

- Rice – Bhaat
- Bread – Rotli/ Parotha/ Thepla/Bhakri
- Milk – Doodh
- Vegetables – Shaakbhaji
- Lentils – Daal
- Fruits – Fal (/Fad)
- Sweets – Mithai/ Gadyu
- Snacks – Naasto

Let's eat! - Chalo jamva!

Dining Table Phrases

- What's for dinner today? – Aaje jamvama shu chhe?

- I want water. – Mane pani joiye chhe.

- This food tastes very good. – Jamvanu bahu swadisht chhe.

- Can I have more? – Mane vadhare malse/ mali shake?

- Eat your food. – Tamaru jamvanu jamo/ Jamvanu jamilo.

- I don't like this. – Mane aa nathi gamtu / Mane na bhavyu.

- It's very spicy. – Bahu teekhu chhe.

Image by brgfx on Freepik

Let's go play! – Chalo ramva jaiye!

Playing Outside

- Let's go outside. – Chalo bahar jaiye.
- I want to play. – Mane ramvu chhe.
- Be careful! – Dhyaan rakho! / Sambhalo (/Sambhado)!
- It's time to go home. – Ghare javano samay thai gayo chhe.
- Did you enjoy? – Tamne/tane maja aavi?
- It's my turn now. – Havey maaro varo chhe.
- Don't fight! – Lado nai! /Jagadvanu nai!
- I want to play on the swing. – Mare jhula (swing) par ramvu chhe.
- I want to play on the slide. – Mare lapasni (slide) par ramvu chhe.

Chit chatting with friends!
- Mitro saathe vaat chit !

Conversations with Friends

- What are you (all) doing? – Tame shu kari rahya chho?/ Tame shu karo chho?

- Let's meet in the evening. – Chalo saanje maliye.

- I missed you! – Mae tamne bahu yaad karya! / Tamari bahu yaad aavi!

- Let's watch a movie together. – Chalo saathe movie joiye.

- Will you have some tea/ coffee? – Cha/ coffee lesho?

- Let's meet for lunch! – Lunch karva maliye!

Image by grmarc / Freepik

**Thank you for being my friend.
– Mari mitra/bahenpani (female) banva mate aabhar (/thank you).**

Conversations with Friends

- Are you okay? – Tame theek chho? / Tu theek chhe?

- I am not okay. – Hu theek nathi.

- Tell me what happened. – Mane kehe/kaho shu thayu.

- Don't worry, everything will be fine. – Chinta na karo, badhu saru thashe.

- Thank you for being my friend. – Maro/mari mitra banva mate aabhar.

I want dhokla and samosa!
– Mane dhokla ane samosa joiye chhe.

Conversations with Relatives (2)

- How are you, uncle? – Kaka (uncle), tame kem chho?

- How are you, aunty? – Kaki (aunty), tame kem chho?

- How is your family? – Tamara ghare badha kem chhe?

- It's been a long time since we met. – Bahu samay thai gayo apanane/tamne malye.

- Please visit our home. – Amara ghare aavjo.

- Let's eat together. – Chalo saathe jamiye.

Let's pray and do puja.
– Chalo prarthna ane puja kariye.

Conversations with Relatives (2)

- You are looking nice. – Tame sundar lago chho.

- Who made this food? – Aa jamvanu kone banavyu?

- Let's take a family photo. – Chalo ek family photo laiye.

- The kids are playing outside. – Chokrao / balako bahar rami rahya chhe.

- When will we meet again? – Aapne fari kyare malishu?

I want to ride in a rickshaw.
– Mane rickshaw ma besvu chhe.

Traveling in a Taxi/Rickshaw

- I need a taxi/rickshaw. – Mane ek taxi/rickshaw joiye chhe.

- How much will it cost? – Ana ketla rupiya/paisa thase?

- Please drive slowly. – Krupa karine dhime chalavo.

- Stop here. – Ahiya roko.

- Thank you for the ride. – Savari mate aabhar.

Image by pikisuperstar on Freepik

**We are going on a trip.
– Ame farva jaiye chiye.**

Traveling (Airport)

- Where is the boarding gate? – Boarding gate kya chhe?

- I have two bags. – Mari paase be bag chhe.

- What time is the flight? – Flight kyare chhe? /Flight ketla vage chhe?

- Can I get a window seat? – Mane ek window seat mali shake?

- Let's go to security check. – Chalo security check ma jaiye.

Let's go to the market to buy groceries.
– Chalo market ma shak bhaji leva jaiye.

Asking for Help

- Can you help me, please? – Tame mari madad karsho?

- I am lost. – Hu khovai gayi / gayo chhu.

- Please call the doctor. – Krupaya doctor ne bolavo.

- I need some water. – Mane thodu pani joiye chhe.

- Thank you for helping me. – Mane madad karva mate aabhar.

Image by prostooleh on Freepik

I want to draw a rainbow – Mare indradhanush (rainbow) dorvu chhe.

A rainbow has seven colors – Indradhanush ma saat rango chhe.

Hobbies and Interests (1)

- I like reading books. – Mane pustako (/books) vanchvano shokh chhe.

- I love to sing. – Mane gaavu gamey chhe.

- Do you play any instruments? – Tame koi vaajintro (/instrument) vagado chho?

- Let's draw / paint together. – Chalo saathe chitra doriye/ (paint kariye).

- My favorite hobby is dancing. – Maro gamto shokh nrutya (/dancing) chhe./ Mane dance karvo gamey chhe.

Image by freepik

I like to play video games.
– Mane video games ramvi gamey chhe.

Hobbies and Interests (2)

- What's your favorite movie? – Tamaru gamtu (/ favorite) movie kayu chhe?

- Let's watch a comedy (movie). – Chalo ek comedy film joiye.

- The movie was amazing! – Movie jabardast hatu!

- Do you like action films? – Tamne action filmo gamey chhe?

- Let's go to the theater tomorrow. – Chalo avtikale theater jaiye.

I turned nine years old!
– Hoon nav varsh no thayo!
(/Hu nav varsh ni thai)

Birthday

- Happy Birthday! – Janmadivas ni shubhkamnao!

- How old are you? – Tame ketla varsh na thaya?/ Tamari ummar ketli chhe?

- Let's cut the cake. – Chalo cake kapiye.

- Where's the party? – Party kya chhe?

- Did you like your gift? – Tamne tamari gift gami? / Tane tari gift gami?

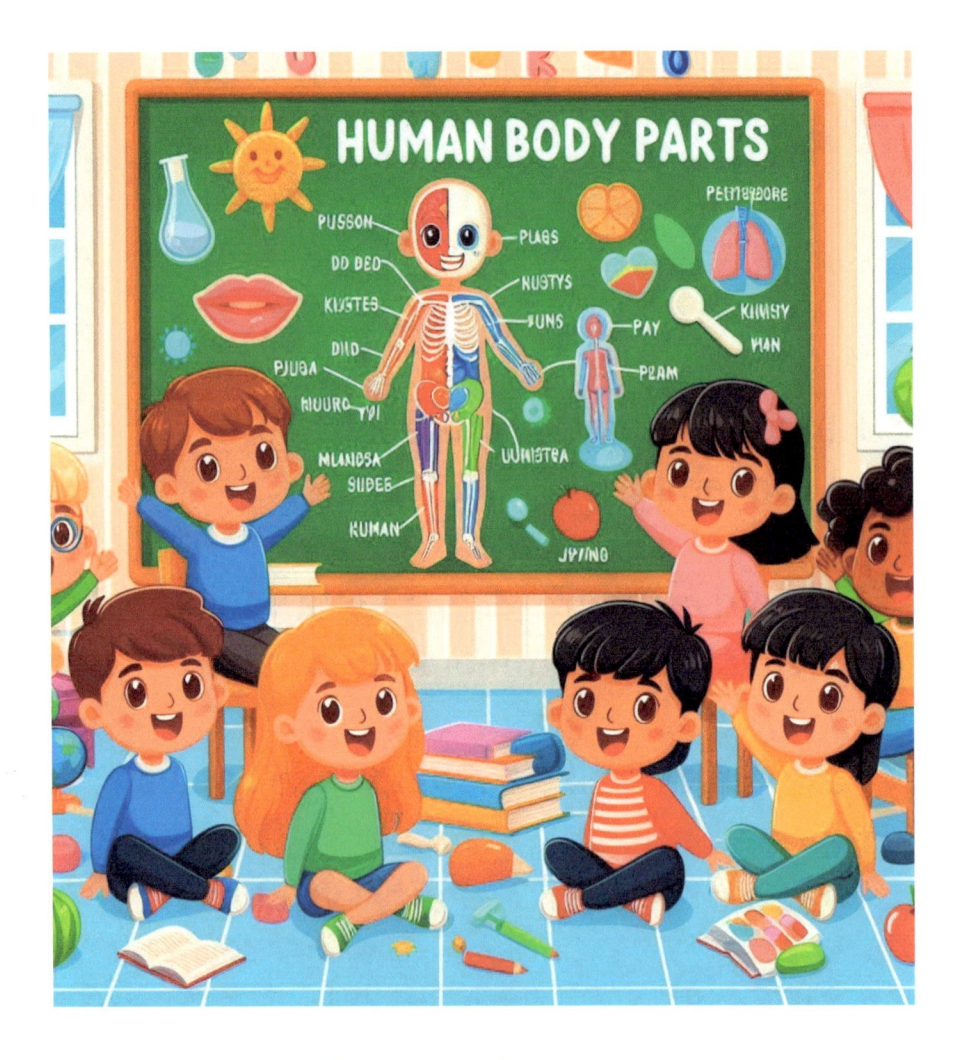

I have ten fingers.
– Mari paase das aanglio (/aangdio) chhe.

Let's learn something new.
– Chalo kaik navu shikhiye.

Body Parts

- Head – Maathu
- Hair – Vaal (/Vaad)
- Forehead – Kapal (/Kapad)
- Eyes – Aankh
- Ears – Kan
- Nose – Naak
- Mouth – Modhu
- Teeth – Daant
- Lips – Hoth
- Tongue – Jeebh
- Neck – Galu (/Gadu)
- Shoulder – Khabho
- Hand – Haath
- Fingers – Aangliyo (/ Aangdio)
- Chest – Chhati
- Stomach – Paet
- Back – Pith
- Leg – Pag
- Knee – Ghutan
- Foot – Pag nu Taliyu

Image by Harryarts on Freepik

**Let's play dandiya!
– Chalo dandiya ramiye!**

Festivals

- Happy Diwali! – Diwali ni shubhkamnao!

- Let's light the lamps. – Chalo diva pragtaviye.

- I want to fly a kite. – Mane patang chagaavavi chhe.

- Let's play garba during Navratri. – Navratri ma garba ramva jaiye.

- Let's make a rangoli. – Chalo rangoli banaviye.

- Let's play Holi. – Chalo Holi (/dhuleti) ramiye.

It's very sunny today.
– Aaje bahu tadko chhe.

It's raining a lot today.
- Aaje bahu varsad pade chhe / aave chhe.

Describing the Weather

- It is hot today. – Aaje garami chhe.

- It is cold today. – Aaje thandi chhe.

- I like winter. – Mane shiyalo (/shiyado) gamey chhe.

- It's raining outside. – Bahar varsad aave chhe / Bahar varsad pade chhe.

- Let's go out in the sun. – Chalo bahar tadka ma jaiye.

- It's so cold! – Bahu thandi chhe!

- It is windy today. – Aaje bahu pavan chhe.

Our family has a cat.
– Mara parivar (family) paase ek biladi chhe.

I'm scared of the lion.
– Mane sinh thi dar/beek lage.

Animals

- Dog – Kutro
- Cat – Biladi
- Rabbit – Saslu
- Fish – Machali
- Bird – Pakshi/ Panki
- Lion – Sinh
- Elephant – Haathi
- Tiger – Vaagh
- Deer – Haran
- Bear – Rinch
- Monkey – Vaandro
- Fox – Shiyaal (/Shiyaad)
- Horse – Ghodo
- Camel – Oont
- Donkey – Gadhedo

My favorite color is red.
– Maro maangamto rang laal chhe.

Colors and Shapes

- Red – Laal
- Blue – Bhuro/ Vaadli
- Green – Lilo
- Yellow – Pilo (/Pido)
- Black – Kaalo (/Kaado)
- White – Safed
- Pink – Gulabi
- Orange – Naarangi
- Brown – Kaathai

- Circle – Vartul/ Gol (/Goad)
- Square – Choras
- Triangle – Trikon
- Rectangle – Lumbchoras
- Oval – Andakaar

It was nice meeting you all!
- Tamne badhane maline maja aavi!

Saying Goodbye

- Goodbye, see you later. – Aavjo, pachhi maliye.

- Take care of yourself! – Tabiyat sachavjo!

- See you tomorrow. – (Avti) kale maliye.

- Have fun! – Maja karjo!

- I'll call you soon. – Hu jaldi tamne call karish.

- I will miss you. – Hu tamne/tane yaad karish.

- We'll meet again soon. – Aapne jaldi maliye.

- Safe travels! – Tamari yatra sukhad rahe!

End Note

As a mother of two little ones, creating this book was a heartfelt journey. My goal was simple—to make it easier for families, especially those living abroad, to help their children speak and understand Gujarati with confidence. Language is more than just words; it's a bridge to our culture, roots, and heritage.

I know firsthand how challenging it can be to pass on a native language when surrounded by a different linguistic environment. That's why I designed this book with simple, easy-to-use translations, making learning Gujarati fun and accessible for kids and parents alike. Whether you're teaching your little ones their first words, helping them connect with grandparents, or just keeping your culture alive at home, I hope this book becomes a helpful resource in your journey.

Thank you for allowing me to be a small part of your family's language-learning experience. May this book bring joy, connection, and a love for Gujarati into your home!

Lastly, I want to acknowledge Krina Patel, Ankit Patel and Preeti Gajjr for their valuable input in making this book better!

With love and gratitude,
- Drashti

Made in United States
Cleveland, OH
28 May 2025